Untold Credit Repair Strategies Revealed

Your Guide to Reclaiming Your Credit

By Latrice Douglas

www.wealthyrise.com
Printed in the United States of America

Disclaimer:

Those of us at Wealthy Rise Credit Solutions are not lawyers. The contents of this book should not be considered legal advice in any way. This book is from the perspective of the author and based on actual research and knowledge from a licensed professional. You are solely responsible for any actions taken, or not taken based on the material provided. If you agree, please continue. Wealthy Rise Credit Solutions, LLC expressly disclaims all warranties as to the contents of this publication, including, without, the implied warranties of merchantability, fitness for a particular purpose, infringement, and makes no warranty as to the results that may be achieved by using the information contained in this publication. This information can be used in a variety of ways to fit various purposes, and Wealthy Rise Credit Solutions, LLC will not be responsible for any damages (including, without limitation, indirect, consequential, special, or punitive damages) suffered or incurred by any person reading this book.

"I believe we all deserve to live out our dreams and live the best life possible. I am a woman of many hats with no limits. I am blessed to help others. I have helped so many people, and it fills my heart with joy! Cheers to better credit, building wealth and a better future. I look forward to helping you get there!" -Latrice Douglas

This book is dedicated to all of my family and friends – my parents, sisters, my son and his family which is now my family. I love you all very much and I want to thank everyone for all of their support.

TABI

About the Author:

I am Latrice Douglas. An entrepreneur, a single mother, and a trailblazer for women who wish to crawl from underneath the depths of their financial struggles. Three years ago, I had a credit score of 355 and was in desperate need of a vehicle for me and my child. With a low credit score, and being a single parent, my options were limited. I ended up purchasing a 2007 Toyota

Corolla with an interest rate of 22%. I was spending more than what the car was worth, and it was because of my credit. That was the cherry on top of the financial cake for me, as I knew I needed to make a change, and I knew exactly where I needed to start.

I've had a background in banking for seven years, getting a job in the industry at just nineteen years old. Growing up in a military family, my parents were far from financially illiterate, raising me to be the best woman I could become. While they weren't well versed on the ins and outs of credit in general, my mother taught me the basics of credit card responsibility at a young age. She always told me to borrow only what I needed, and to pay it back on time every month. Basic knowledge like that is a stepping stone toward putting your children on the right path of maintaining good credit throughout adulthood. Unfortunately, life has its way of throwing curve balls at us. Sometimes a bad situation can be the beginning of a crippling credit score. We can't always control what life throws at us, but we can control how we pull ourselves up, to get back on track.

While working full time in a Human Resources position, I started reading books on how to repair my credit. This led to me making the decision to become an entrepreneur, and I became a certified credit repair agent through Mark Clayborne. Mark is a well renowned credit repair business coach who helps aspiring entrepreneurs start their own credit repair businesses. He trains them in basic and advanced credit repair that includes how to start a credit repair business, software training on how to master the credit repair software in less than a week, and various ways to market your credit repair business and generate massive leads. I was so thankful that he put me on the right path and helped me become the professional business woman I am today. I couldn't have done it without his help, and I used everything he taught me to build Wealthy Rise Credit Solutions, LLC.

Wealthy Rise made its debut in August of 2017, with three employees and over 170 customers. There are no third parties with us, and we offer nothing but honesty and transparency to make sure our clients are satisfied. My goal is to educate you, in hopes that you find the information given in this book useful and use it as a learning tool to help yourself.

Chapter 1: The Importance of Your Credit

One of the main contributors to a life of bad credit, is financial illiteracy. From a young age, most low-income Americans raise their children with the idea that anything involving credit is a scam. They tell them to avoid credit cards, and to pay for most things in cash. While paying for things in cash is never a bad idea, the misconception that credit cards are not beneficial, is. Having no credit score is essentially just as bad as having a bad score. A bad credit score controls where you live, and how much you pay for things. Bad credit leads to income inequality, and the inability to get ahead. You can't rent apartments, buy homes or qualify for loans. Establishing credit is essential, and is necessary for everyone, no matter your lifestyle. Without a good credit score, you will end up paying more in interest for things such as car notes. Don't end up like I did, paying more than what my car was worth, which will be like throwing money into the garbage.

Depending on the type of job you have, many employers conduct credit checks as a part of the hiring process. If you haven't demonstrated financial responsibility, a prospective employer might be hesitant to hire you. For example, the employer might believe your level of debt is too high for the salary offered. Some employers also check credit scores before giving a promotion or raise, especially for financial-related or executive positions.

There are many ways to build and maintain a credit score. There are also ways that late or missed payments can negatively affect your credit, but don't necessarily increase your score. In this chapter I will explain how credit scores work and are calculated, and the difference between credit scores and credit reports.

How A Credit Score Is Calculated

Since most credit scoring systems are based on a creditor's individual experience with customers, they are unique for each customer. To develop a system, the creditor selects a random sample of its customers and performs a statistical analysis. They identify customers who have demonstrated the characteristics of being credit worthy. From the list of those identified, they use different factors to determine who would be a good credit risk. 35% of your credit score is your history. It is the most important factor in an increasing or decreasing credit score. Next is your amounts owed, which represents 30%, and is calculated by comparing the amount of money that is owed to how much can still be borrowed from the same lender. As an example, if you have a credit card with a $4,000 credit limit and you have charged $2,000, that would give you a debt to available credit ratio of 50%. This will decrease your score. Anything over 30% will because calculated and reported debts in any given month drops your score until it is paid down below 30%. It is recommended that you keep it below 30% to maintain a good score. 15% of your score is the length of time your account has been open. It takes time to build a great credit score. A small dip in numbers may be due to an account being new which also accounts for 10% of your score. The final 10% is the type of credit used, which is demonstrating that you can handle different types of loans, whether it's a revolving loan, such as a credit card, or an installment loan such as an auto loan. Always keep these things in mind when handling your credit accounts.

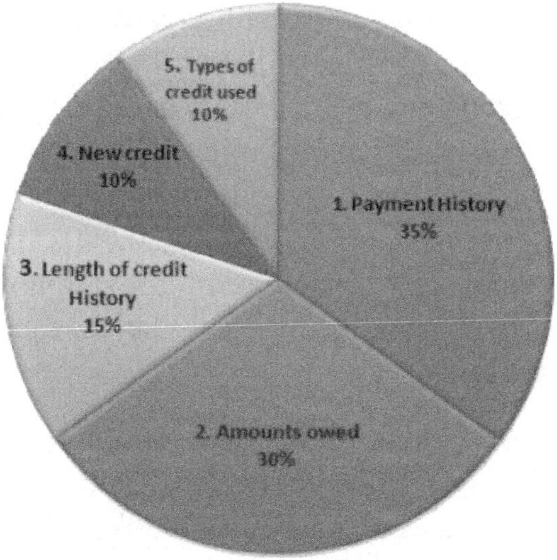

Fico Credit Score Factors

A Thorough Look into What Makes Your Credit Rise and Fall

Old negative items in your credit report can cause your credit to decrease. Examples of these negative items include foreclosure, bankruptcy or late payments. If one, or all of these have remained on your credit file for a few years, your credit score will be affected. Fluctuations in credit balances can also be a factor. Whether or not you are paying off your balances in full, your credit card balance is bound to change on a monthly basis since you make use of it frequently. Additionally, your credit utilization goes up as your balances go up.

Credit utilization is the result you obtain when you divide the amount of debt on your credit card by your credit limit. For instance, one of your credit cards has a balance of $10,000, and you have a $20,000 limit in credit, your credit utilization is 0.5 (that is, 10,000/20,000 = 0.5), or if you prefer, 50%. Your credit utilization changes every month since your balance changes every month.

The age of your credit history is also another factor. Your score can improve as your credit file and account gets older. FICO® looks at both your oldest account and the average age of your accounts. When your accounts cross an age barrier that FICO® finds very important, this factor can cause your score to increase, although it might have no significance in a specific month. Applying for new credit, such as applying for different credit cards within the span of a few months, is never a good idea, and will most likely drop your score.

Try to keep a lookout for updates in the FICO® rating methods. In order to make their rating a more precise index of credit risk, FICO® updates its rating methods on a continuous basis. Hence, different rating methods can be applied to your credit file within a specific period of time. Thus, your score can change when an updated rating method is applied to your credit file. ***Pro Tip:**

Chapter 2: Steps Toward Building or Rebuilding Your Credit

As mentioned in the previous chapter, there are sites where you can check your credit for free such as **www.annualcreditreport.com.** A vital part of a credit report is for you to get a copy of the report. It is important that you obtain and review your report at least once in a year, even if you are sure that your credit is strong. What most people aren't aware of, is that by law the *Fair Credit Reporting Act* states that credit reporting agencies must give you a free copy of your credit report at least once in a year, provided you ask for it. But you can still obtain additional credit reports if and when necessary from other agencies. When you want to obtain your credit report, provide the credit reporting agency with your personal information. I know that this is something people often hesitate to do, not wanting these agencies to have their current address, but it is a necessary step in getting your credit report. During the process of entering your personal information, it is highly recommended that you check the box which instructs the agency not to include the first 5 digits of your social security number on the report they will send to you.

Contact the annual credit report service through annualcreditreport.com to get your free report from either Experian, Equifax, or Transunion. Be sure to ignore those pesky advertisements for additional services, such as, credit monitoring or paying for a credit score.

***PRO TIP make sure you use the exact URL as specified, www.annualcreditreports.com. Beware of phony businesses who will try to squeeze cash from you by using similar names and URLs.** Be careful of emails and pop-ups that claim to offer free reports, they are only after your personal information. You won't be asked to provide your personal information, either by email or phone call from the credit reporting agency.

You may also request an additional credit report for free based on your credit, if your credit was denied, you were unable to get credit on the terms you requested, your credit account has been halted or if there have been unfavorable changes to your account by a creditor, without the same changes being applied to other customer accounts of the same type. Before a creditor takes any of the actions mentioned, you must be told the name and address of the credit reporting agency. Once you know the credit reporting agency, request your report from them within 60 days from the time any of the conditions above was applied to

WebBank/Fingerhut Advantage. This account lets you shop more often, build credit with the major monitoring agencies, and potentially qualify for credit line increases and other perks.

Walmart credit cards are also great for those looking to rebuild their credit score. You can save money by taking advantage of their many discounts, and they offer free FICO® and TransUnion score when you opt to receive online statements. Cardholders also have the option to withdraw up to $100 in cash at their stores when making a purchase. Unlike other companies, withdrawing cash counts as a purchase. So, you don't have to worry about fees or interest charges as long as the balance is paid in full on time each month.

Allow me to let you in on a little secret. Have you ever heard of the shopping cart trick? The shopping cart trick is a clever method that allows people with bad credit to get a credit card. The shopping cart trick relies on the fact that many websites will pre-approve you for a credit card during the checkout process without actually checking your score. But there are a few things you must know before attempting this trick. You must opt-in for credit card offers. Turn off your popup blocker or anti-spam tool so credit card offers can appear on your screen. Do not enter your full social security number. It is recommended that you only enter the last four digits. Only works with Comenity Bank. There are plenty of stores that have Comenity credit cards, and below is a list of those stores:

Abercrombie & Fitch
Ann Taylor
Bath & Body Works
Brylane Home
Buckle Coldwater
Express
GameStop
HSN
J.Crew
Jessica London
JJill
King Size Direct
Loft
Motorola
MyPoints
New York & Company
One Stop Plus
Overstock
PacSun
Romans
Sportsman Guide
Total Rewards
Venus
Victoria's Secret
Wayfair

1. https://www.selflender.com/ - It's a savings account that reports as a 1k installment loan to all 3 bureau on your credit report. Most of my clients see an increase of at least 30 points just by signing up in 45 days! It's just $12 to start, you get all of your money back plus interest at the end of the year.

information each month, your credit report changes.

Negotiating

Negotiate with each of your creditors and if both of you are able to reach an agreement, pay off the debts of the one with the most favorable agreement first. If you can't pay off everything at once, start paying their debts first. Choose the card where the amount you owe is the minimum. Thus, you can pay off your debt completely from this and move to the next. This has a positive psychological effect. Select the card with the highest interest rate. This will lower the interest you will pay since you will complete the payments within a few months. Rebuild good credit on the card you want to keep. Make sure to do what is best for you and keep a clear head when negotiating with creditors. Never let your creditor intimidate you into diverting the money you intend to use for bringing your car payments up-to-date to pay your credit card debt. Also, do not agree to pay more than what you can afford. If they think that you can pay $150, then, they will insist that you pay more. Don't accept their demands. If you can't decide immediately, end the call and reschedule to speak with them another time.

You should also find out about using your creditor's waiver. If your bank offers to waive 3 months' interest provided you pay the principal due on your loan, it is only logical for you to ask if the bank is willing to give up 4 or 5 months' interest as well. If you don't ask, you don't get. Ask first! Ask to speak to someone else in a higher authority than the first person you meet, if the first person does not have the authority to make the changes you want. If necessary, speak to the person with the highest authority in the company. Be confident and never let intimidation stop you from getting things done. Never agree to a split! Your creditor may propose that you split the difference between a higher demand and your offer when you proposed a low amount to settle your debt. Don't agree to split the difference, rather, propose an amount between this difference and your original offer. If you pay a lump sum, most creditors are willing to settle for less than the total debt. But if you pay on a monthly, bi-monthly or weekly basis, they will insist you make a full payment. Ensure that the creditor signs a release, and you receive a copy of that release stating that your partial payment excuses you from paying the remaining balance, provided you reached an agreement for you to pay less than the full amount you owe.

When negotiating, beware of the scare tactics used by them. One of the common tactics by collection agencies or creditors is to threaten that they will report you to a credit reporting agency. Don't fall for this tactic and more importantly, do not let this threat change your debt repayment plan. The truth is there is a high probability that your account has already been reported. The reason is that most creditors use an automated system which reports all accounts to credit reporting agencies more than once per month. In actual fact, there are collection agencies that do not report to any credit reporting agency at all. Thoroughly read all the contract of your negotiation, especially if the creditor or collection agency has agreed to all your terms and conditions for repayment. **Pro tip: any time you reach an agreement for a change in payment terms, whether temporary, lump sum or permanent, be sure you fully understand any new credit terms and can afford to make the payments required by a new agreement.** If there is any part of the contract you do not understand, no matter how little, do not sign. Either consult with your lawyer or a credit counselor. **Visit my website www.wealthyrise.com or visit Facebook.com today and join my group, *Building Credit & Wealth*, so you can be a part of a community that keeps you on the right track.** Another common tactic employed by creditors is to agree to all your terms, but then they will ask you to get a cosigner. A cosigner is held responsible when you do not pay your debt even when your debt has been erased through bankruptcy. Any time you reach an agreement for a change in payment terms, whether temporary, lump sum or permanent, be sure you fully understand any new credit terms and can afford to make the payments required by a new agreement.

Negotiating can start at 30% when negotiating with collectors. Make sure you get the entire agreement with them in writing and If you are paying the full amount, negotiate for a "pay for deletion". Get that in writing before you agree to it. If you are paying in full, you want them to delete the negative item in exchange for your payment in full.

Understanding Your Public Record

Public records are very damaging to your credit score. Most people don't know that all of these items can be deleted, and my business has gotten them deleted for clients under the Fair Credit Reporting Act by finding errors, outdated information or information that they can't verify on any given account. They include tax liens, bankruptcies, repossessions, or judgements. Anything where a court was involved. A tax lien is a lien imposed by law upon a property to secure the payment of taxes. A tax lien may be imposed for delinquent taxes owed on real property or personal property, or as a result of failure to pay income taxes or other taxes. A "discharge" removes the lien from specific property. There are several Internal Revenue Code (IRC) provisions that determine eligibility. "Subordination" does not remove the lien but allows other creditors to move ahead of the IRS, which may make it easier to get a loan or mortgage. A "withdrawal" removes the public Notice of Federal Tax Lien and assures that the IRS is not competing with other creditors for your property; however, you are still liable for the amount due. A lien attaches to all of your assets (such as property, securities, vehicles) and to future assets acquired during the duration of the lien. Once the IRS files a Notice of Federal Tax Lien, it may limit your ability to get credit. The lien attaches to all business property and to all rights to business property, including accounts receivable. If you file for bankruptcy, your tax debt, lien, and Notice of Federal Tax Lien may continue after the bankruptcy. A lien is often confused with a Levy, but they are not the same. A levy actually takes the property to pay the tax debt. If you don't pay or make arrangements to settle your tax debt, the IRS can levy, seize and sell any type of real or personal property that you own or have an interest in.

Bankruptcy is a legal status of a person or other entity that cannot repay debts to creditors. In most jurisdictions, bankruptcy is imposed by a court order, often initiated by the debtor. Any individual, even if self-employed or operating an unincorporated business, is eligible for chapter 13 relief as long as the individual's unsecured debts are less than $394,725 and secured debts are less than $1,184,200. These amounts are adjusted periodically to reflect changes in the consumer price index. A corporation or partnership may not be a chapter 13 debtor. An individual cannot file under chapter 13 or any other chapter if, during the preceding 180 days, a prior bankruptcy petition was dismissed due to the debtor's willful failure to appear before the court or comply with orders of the court or was voluntarily dismissed after creditors sought relief from the bankruptcy court to recover property upon which they hold liens. Bankruptcy can temporarily stop a foreclosure, tax lien, repossession or eviction. It can also stop creditor harassment and collection activities. Bankruptcy cannot prevent a secured creditor from foreclosing or repossessing property you can't afford. It also cannot eliminate student loans, alimony and child support obligations.

Repossession is a term used to denote a financial institution taking back an object that was either used as collateral or rented or leased. When you buy a car, truck, or other vehicle on credit, you should be aware that until you have made the last payment your creditor retains important rights in the vehicle. These rights are established by the contract you signed and by the laws of your state. Most consumers know that repossession means losing the collateral you put up to secure a loan, things like a car, home, land, or personal property. What you might not know is the problems don't stop there. Repossession leaves a negative mark on your credit history and damage your credit score. a one-two punch that can cripple your finances and limit your ability to get affordable financing in the future. Repossessions stay on your credit report for seven years. While they can have a huge negative impact on your credit score, it lessens over time, and is wiped out completely after the seven-year mark.

A judgement is a court order that gives a creditor the legal right to collect from a debtor. Many judgments will contain an order of payments. The court's rules or state statutes may require that you be allowed to pay the judgment in installments. But an installment order does not carry a requirement that you receive a periodic statement like a credit card or loan. You can pay the judgment. You can attempt to negotiate a settlement for the judgment amount. You can file bankruptcy and discharge the judgment. Or you can do nothing and let the judgment creditor forcefully collect.

What You Need to Know About ChexSystems

ChexSystems is similar to the big three credit bureaus, except its main focus is your checking and savings account, instead of your credit history. I know what you're probably thinking, "There's more I need to worry about?!?" But don't worry, I've got you covered. While ChexSystems may seem intimidating, it's pretty easy to understand. Here are the eight things you should know about the ChexSystems to ensure you'll never be rejected for a checking or a savings account:

1. You can get your free report every year. Visit **www.ChexSystems.com** so you can spot ID Theft or bank errors early.

2. You can dispute incorrect information at www.ChexSystems.com as well.

3. If you ever open a checking or savings account, you automatically have a ChexSystems report.

4. At **www.consumerfinance.gov/complaint/** you can use the CFPB if you have a complaint.

5. If you can't open a checking account because of Chex, consider getting a "Fresh Start" checking account, offered by some banks such as Wells Fargo.

6. Bouncing checks or not paying back your overdrafts can get you on the negative list.

7. Once you are on the negative list, it can take five years to get off.

8. Being on the negative list makes it difficult for you to open a new checking or savings accounts.

ChexSystems provides your risk score and your risk report to banks. Your scores range from 100 to 899. The higher your score, the better, since high scores show that you're a less risky customer. Your report shows items such as unpaid fees, which usually are a result of over drafting. Bounced checks from retailers and also suspected fraud. Reports also list credit inquiries, check orders and consumer-initiated security freezes. If you have ever been a victim of identity theft, you can put a freeze on your report. This way, no new accounts can be approved without your authorization. You can request both your score and your report at the agency. I recommend the report, that way, you get more useful information as to why a bank may have rejected you. It takes about five business days to receive your report, but you might not find much on it. But consider that a relief. Unlike credit reports, ChexSystems reports only focus on the negative. If there is no negative to report, then you are all good!

Credit & Student Loans

After your college graduation, repaying a loan quickly, without any missed or late payments is a great way to build and keep a good credit score. Resolve any delinquencies as soon as you can, do not wait. However, there are a number of things to be careful of. Paying off your student loan early may have a negative effect on your credit score. Student loans are installment loans which, unlike credit card debt, it does not look good to creditors to have the lowest balance possible. Future creditors understand that a student loan means there is no larger balance of available credit and that your monthly payment will not change over the lifetime of the loan.

Resolve any delinquency as soon as urgently as you can. Although I stated that paying it off too quickly can damage your score, leaving it delinquent in hopes to pay it off later is much more damaging. Student loans taken out with a private lender have fewer repayment options than a federal student loan. What you must do in the case of dealing with a private lender, is notify them before you miss a payment to set up a new payment plan. If it is too late for you to do this, then you will need to establish a new repayment plan quickly and follow up with the lender and the credit reporting agencies to make sure any bad information about it has been updated to show a repayment plan is now in place. Although student loans are below other types of loans when it comes to damaging your credit score, it is still important to keep them on the right track.

When it comes to Deferring your student loans, it will not hurt your credit score. Opting to defer on student loans, while not as ideal as repaying them because all it does, is delay the inevitable, it won't hurt your credit score. In fact, financial institutions may take your deferment into account when deciding whether or not to approve you for a loan. Lenders may come to the conclusion that you have enough money to pay back the loan they are offering, since part of your income wouldn't have to go toward repaying student loans immediately. You can contact the student loan company that you have your loans through and request to see if you qualify for any student loan forgiveness programs. Many industries such as government, public services etc. qualify to make nine on time payments and have the rest of the student loan forgiven. Please do your research to see if you qualify. if not, then you have other options as well. An income-based repayment plan, or a deferment for 6 months or so if you have lost your job or do not make enough money to cover your loan payment. One single 30-day late payment can drop your credit score up to 80 points each.

Repossessions

Sometimes we purchase a shiny new car, and everything seems great. Then all of a sudden, life happens. You lose your job, or your family becomes financially burdened by illness. Your ability to afford this new car is stripped away, and now your vehicle is facing repossession. Repossession is a term used to denote a financial institution taking back an object that was either used as collateral or rented or leased. Repossession is a "self-help" type of action in which the party having the right of ownership of the property in question takes the property back from the party having the right of possession without invoking court proceedings. This will usually mean substantial damage to your credit.

According to Experian, auto repossessions stay on your credit report for up to seven years. When you stop making payments and lose your car, this does not mean your financial responsibility for that car is over. If the car is auctioned off for less than your outstanding loan balance, then you would still owe a deficiency balance. You could also buy back the vehicle at auction and pay any repossession fees, but most people who are dealing with an auto repossession, cannot afford to do that. Here are three major tips you can use to avoid repossession or fix your credit after it happens.

The first thing you can do, is find an attorney. If you're tempted to stop making payments because you feel misled about the condition of the car, don't. In most cases, an attorney can help you resolve the issue rather than having your credit dinged by a repossession. You can also try to negotiate with your auto lender. Before you decide to stop making payments, call the financing company to discuss your situation. They may extend your loan, in hopes of getting the money back if they feel that you can actually pay it back. If you need another vehicle to get to work while you're rebuilding your credit, Auto attorneys suggest looking at financing companies that provide financing to people who've had past repossessions. The interest rates are usually higher since it’s a higher risk loan but making payments on a new auto loan could help repair your credit.

Chapter 4: Disputing Your Credit Information

According to the **Fair Credit Reporting Act**, you have the right to dispute all incorrect, outdated, unverifiable, and/or missing information in your credit file by law. The credit reporting agency must either reinvestigate or delete the items you dispute from your credit report once they receive your letter. The credit bureaus by law have 30 days to respond to you on an investigation with changes, updates, or deletions. After an item has been deleted from your credit report, the credit reporting agency must give you a notification by telephone, send a written follow-up confirmation and also send a copy of your new credit report at most 5 days after the items have been deleted. As mentioned in a previous Part, there is a statute of limitations in some states regarding how long items can remain on your credit history. This is vital information, and one of the things I stress the most when trying to repair your credit.

Conducting an Investigation

Within 5 business days of receiving your dispute letter, the agency must get in touch with the creditor that sent the information you are disputing by sending them all the relevant information you've submitted. Within 5 business days of completing its investigation, the agency must inform you of their conclusion and if any changes were made. Then they must send you a new credit report within that 5 business days period. The investigation must be concluded within 30 days. But if you send additional relevant information to the agency, the investigation can be extended to 45 days.

Sometimes, a reporting agency can do a "rush" investigation if you pre-inform them that you intend to obtain a mortgage or car loan. Keep in mind that it costs nothing for you to request for a reinvestigation. Though you are allowed to submit your dispute online by the three major credit reporting agencies, I highly recommend that you use direct mail, especially when your dispute requires documentation. For example, you need to provide a letter of claim abandonment, canceled check, or a statement of an account with a zero balance. But for general issues that do not require any documentation, you may submit your dispute online. After a thorough examination of your report, compile a list of the missing and wrong detail. Then write a letter which identifies the parts where corrections are to be made and the reasons why those corrections need to be made.

Letters to Request Removal & Tips for Sending Them

When writing a letter to request removal, be sure to start off by telling them your reason for the letter. Be sure to include the date that you received a copy of your credit report, followed by a list of the information that is incorrect. Let them know that you requested that the credit bureau remove that information from your file, and that the bureau has refused.

Unless you have supplied more information, the creditor is not obligated to deal with the same dispute again. But if you can provide proof that the investigation was not properly conducted, then you need to keep following up on your complaints until the creditor company responds. If you do not receive any response to your letters, take other aggressive steps. You can go to the creditor's company. Sit down at their customer service department, with vice president of marketing, with the CEO or even in the president's office until someone attends to you. It is one of your rights to demand attention. If the creditor has admitted to its own mistakes, obtain a letter from them and send a copy of this letter to the credit reporting agency.

Filing a Complaint

If neither the creditor nor the credit reporting agency is ready to help, you can file your dispute claims with the Federal Trade Commission. To do this, visit www.ftccomplaintassistant.gov, to use their online form. Select **FTC complaint assistant.** If you prefer making phone calls to online assistance, then call the FTC directly at 877-382-4357. Keep in mind that although the government agency does not represent you personally, they may send an inquiry and subsequently take legal actions against the company, if there are sufficient complaints or other proofs of misconducts by the company. However, I do not recommend disputing online because you waive your rights to dispute an account for the same reason if they mark it as verified. You don't want to waive rights, you want to be protected in the event that you may need to sue in court based on facts. This is why I always recommend being honest and using only factual disputing.

If you are in a state with laws that are applicable to credit reporting agencies or creditors who supply information to them, you can file your complaint with the state's attorney general. You can also file your complaint with the consumer protection agency of your state. You have the right to file a brief statement about the dispute if the credit reporting agency's investigation does not resolve the dispute to your satisfaction. In any report that the agency submits, it must include your statement or a summary of your statement. There is no specific word limit, but it is ideal to ensure that the statement is as brief as possible. The reason for this is because the chances of the statement being edited are slim if it is short.

Chapter 5: Common Errors in Your Report

A study by the Federal Trade Commission in 2012 found that 1 in 5 people who examined their credit reports found mistakes and had modifications made. Around 13% of consumers actually had their credit score changed after disputing inaccurate information. And around 5% of all consumers were found to have a mistake that decreased the likelihood of getting approved for a line of credit or a loan. Though errors in credit reports can differ from one individual to another, the following listed are the most common ones:

1. Wrong personal information (name, social security number, or employers) from credit reporting agencies. Your name may be spelled incorrectly. Omission of previous addresses, especially if you have not lived up to 2 years at your current address. Wrong birth date or social security number. Wrong, invalid or missing information about your employment status.

2. Mixed account information might appear on your credit report if you have been a victim of stolen identity.

3. Your ex-spouse's information may be mixed with yours even after you've been divorced.
4. Incorrect payment status of your accounts.
5. Your report may contain multiple dates if an account has been transferred to a debt collector.
6. It seems your creditor closed the account when you were the one who closed the account.
7. Credit reporting agencies failing to acknowledge the accounts in which you no longer have debts to pay.
8. Your spouse, or ex, filed for bankruptcy, but bankruptcy appears in your report, including bankruptcy of more than 10 years.
9. Lawsuits you knew nothing about.
10. Lawsuits and judgments older than 7 years.
11. Tax lien records or criminal records of more than 7 years.
12. Liens reported as unpaid. These include taxes, judgment, or mechanic's payment.

13. Credit a person whose name is similar to yours but who is reported as you.

14. An account for which only your spouse is responsible is listed as joint.

15. Debts which your spouse incurred are listed as yours.

16. Case(s) of stolen identity.

17. An account in your spouse's name, which you are authorized to use, is not reported in your credit report.

18. Wrong account history: you paid on time, but it is reported as a late payment.

19. Your report shows that you still owe a debt for which you have been discharged, or your balance is not zero when you have discharged the debt in bankruptcy.

20. You freely surrendered your vehicle, but it is listed as being repossessed.

21. Missing records of when you disputed a charge on your credit card.

22. Accounts you have closed but are still reported as open (making it seem as if you have a lot of open credit).

23. A co-signatory account of which you know nothing.

24. Wrong dates. Such as the start dates for an account charged off or sent to collection. Similarly, a correct date for one delinquent account and an incorrect one for another delinquent account or wrong dates for when one of your accounts was transferred to a collection agency. Note: when a delinquent account is transferred to a collection agency, the date of delinquency cannot be changed to a new one.

25. Child support of more than 7 years.

26. Dangerous information that is more than 7 years of age.

27. Missing or wrong dates of when you transferred an account from a creditor to a collection agency.

28. Times when you were window shopping. Until you indicate a desire to get credit, it is unlawful for a creditor to pull your credit report without you giving them a written permission to do so.

When any or all of these errors are present in your credit report, your credit limit, score, and other credit terms you may be offered in the future will be affected.

incorrect, the original creditor being incorrect, or the status, charge off amount or balance being wrong, outdated, inaccurate or incorrect. When a credit bureau responds by having "verified" that the inaccurate account is yours, the credit bureau must have a new reason to open a new investigation into the account. This prevents the bureaus from marking the account as frivolous. Credit repair takes time, persistence and a lot of patience. Credit repair companies and professionals should not be guaranteed a specific time frame for you because, as you have learned and will further learn in this book, it is a process. If you do not have the time to do this yourself, then I recommend hiring a professional, but make sure you do your due diligence first.

Difficulty Disputing Errors

Some errors are easy to challenge, and others, unfortunately can be far more difficult. But this is not to steer you away from trying. Despite how easy or hard an error might be to dispute, never give up and give them all you've got! Some items that may be easier to dispute include accounts that are truly not yours, inaccurate late payments, accounts that are outdated, and inaccurate charge-offs. Items that are more difficult to dispute include inaccurate foreclosures, inaccurate repossessions, inaccurate unpaid tax liens and judgments, and inaccurate new late payments which may be up to 90 days old. Many times, the credit bureaus respond to dispute letters by claiming that they verified the item and that you should contact the creditor. Then they include the creditor's contact address and phone number. You should respond back stating that you have already contacted the creditor and have not received a response and hence they should delete the inaccurate item.

Common Mistakes When Disputing

Some credit bureaus, such as TransUnion, still include an arbitration clause in their terms of use. That means if you buy your credit report online and find an error, you can still dispute it. However, if you disagree with how the credit bureau managed the dispute and want to take the bureau to court, the credit bureau can try to press the arbitration clause and force you to give up your right to argue your case before a jury or join in a class-action lawsuit against the bureau. This is also legal for them to try. That can make it even more difficult to prove your case and win considerable damages if you've been financially wronged. In arbitration, your complaint will be handled by an individual arbitrator, appointed from an arbitration association chosen by the credit bureau, and it will be up to the arbitrator to decide your case.

If you disagree with the arbitrator's decision, you are not allowed to appeal. Consumer lawyers have said that "Forced arbitration clauses never help the consumer, and that they only help the business whom are in the wrong. That's another reason why it's beneficial on your part to send your disputes by mail, rather than go through a credit bureau's online system. The issue with online disputes is that you may unintentionally agree to something that can hurt your case by clicking on the wrong thing. By sending your dispute by mail, you'll not only preserve your right to sue, you'll have more control over how much information you can share. Always remember to be brief in any letter that you send. Another mistake that people often make, is not including enough information about your dispute. Consumer lawyers say that using a form supplied by the credit bureau – without attaching additional evidence or a long letter explaining your dispute – could cost you your case if you later need to take the credit bureau to court. So, like I said previously, be brief, but make sure that you are providing enough sufficient information that will be needed to win your case.

Chapter 6: How Credit Agencies Work

Collection agencies make their money off commissions and debts being sold to them. In this case, they collect debts on behalf of creditors. When successful, they remit a specific amount as agreed with the creditor to them. Otherwise, nothing happens. They also make money by buying your debts. For example, assuming the collection agency buys a debt at 8% of its total worth. The collection agency can only recoup their 'investment' if they can convince a customer to go into a payment plan. Assuming the agency collects 25% of the debts they bought, then, they would have made a profit of 17% (without deducting any operating costs they might have incurred in the process). It is important for you to keep in mind that a lot of collection agencies are neither bonded nor do they have the right to collect on a debt. Hence, it is always a good idea to ask for debt validation first.

Credit bureaus use high-end computers that scan each letter looking for signs that your dispute may be frivolous. This is why you would want a human to actually read your letter versus a computer. This can increase the chances of your getting the inaccurate information removed from your report.

Illegal Activity

Under the FDCPA, you can dispute a debt and can also sue the collection agency if it is involved in any or all of the following activities.

The first is communications with third parties. A collection agency must not contact any other person aside from you. The collection agent can only contact another person for the sole purpose of confirming your location. It is illegal for the collection agent to reveal the name of its agency, state that you are a debtor, contact multiple people in order to confirm your location. Except where the response from the first person leads him to the next person or where the response from the first person was completely wrong.

It is important for you to know that the collection agency has the right to contact the credit reporting agency, your original creditor if need be. Only your attorney, provided they know that you have an attorney representing you. Your parents, if you are a minor, and your spouse, if he/she can be properly identified. But if you have told these collection agencies in writing to stop contacting you, they have no right to contact these people.

When communicating with you, it is illegal for the collection agent to contact you if neither the time or place is convenient for you. Generally, it is assumed that calls after 9pm or before are 8am are inconvenient, or if the collector is aware that your boss forbids you to receive collection calls at work.

It is considered harassment if the collector threatens you or another person in a violent manner. If the collector's language is profane, abusive or obscene. If the collector intends to force you to pay by publicly listing your debt for sale or publishing your name in a list of those who do not pay their bills, or false or misleading identification when on the phone, to you or any other person who is receiving the phone call on your behalf.

A collector cannot use false or misleading claims, such as using a badge, sending you a government-issued document or put on a uniform in order to falsely claim to be a law enforcement officer. Present the wrong amount as the amount you owe, or the legal status of your debt. Send you an attorney issued document when it is not an attorney or get your attention by using a fake business name. It is also illegal for them to falsely identify himself to be an employee of the credit or consumer reporting agency. But, he can if the credit or the consumer reporting agency and the debt collector are the same company. Some collectors may also resort to unfair practices that include changing the terms of the original agreement. For example, adding interest fees or charges when he is not authorized. Hoping to threaten you with criminal prosecution by requesting for a postdated check. It is also illegal for a collection agency or an original creditor to change the date of last activity or charge-off so that an item stays on your credit report longer than it should and depositing a posted check before the date on the check or accepting a check postdated by over 5 days. Unless he notifies you in advance of when the check will be deposited.

What to do When They Violate the Law

According to the FDCPA, calling repeatedly or continuously is the most common consumer complaint since 2009. The groups of people who are most vulnerable to illegal practices are the low-income and non-English speaking groups.

it is pretty much guaranteed that collection agents will violate the law. Even the small things that you don't realize are illegal practices. But when this happens, you should know how you can handle it. Regardless of how small the violation may be, always make a clear complaint when a collection agent violates the law. When a collection agent violates the law, you can reach an agreement to cancel some or all of your debt, if you have a witness to back up your claims, have proof of the violation acts, and you file your complaints through the right channels.

You can file your complaint to the creditor if you are convinced that the collection agency is not acting on the orders of the creditor. The Federal Trade Commission (FTC). When you complain to the FTC, attach a copy of your letter to the creditor to the complaint letter which the FTC provides. You should also attach the same letter, if, when you lodge your complaint, you are not using the letter but write a separate letter to the FTC. One of the ways to provide an evidence of the violation is by documenting a log of your phone records. Your state consumer protection office. The procedure for filing a complaint here is similar to filing a complaint with the Federal Trade Commission. You are entitled to damages of up to $1,000 if the agency violates either or all of the Federal Fair Debt Collection Practices Act. Be sure you have a strong case before filing a complaint against a collection agency. For example; if you never hear from a collection agent again after he called more than 5 times in one day, then, you do not have a strong case.

If a Credit Reporting Agency Has Not Removed Your Disputed Information from Your Credit Report

You may need to take a more proactive approach if you believe that you have proof the information in your report is not accurate, but the credit bureau has informed you that the creditor who reported the information is convinced that they sent a verified, accurate and complete information about you and thus they (the credit reporting agency) cannot make any update to your credit report file. Though this response may frustrate you and even take a lot of your time, it is worth the hassle. Contact the creditor associated with the wrong information then, as a matter of urgency, ensure that the creditor informs the agency to remove the wrong information. I highly recommend that you write to the president or CEO of the creditor company if you want immediate attention. Continue sending your 2nd request letter, then send your 3rd round then you can file a complaint with the CFPB and the attorney general and include those copies of the complaint with your round 4 and 5 letters and keep going to round 6, 7, 8, etc. In credit repair it is critical that you are using facts in your disputes. Real errors, that way you can continue to hold the credit bureaus accountable. You can also keep sending the same letters to the original creditor and/or collector at the same time as the credit bureaus for faster results. You have to keep going!

Statute of Limitations by State

Debt falls into four different categories. Oral, written, promissory, and open debt. It is highly recommended to check with your lawyer about which category your debt falls under. An oral agreement simply means that your debt was made based on an oral contract. A written contract was an agreement signed by you and the creditor, that usually comes with specific terms and conditions. A promissory note is an agreement to pay back a debt in payments, an interest rate such as a mortgage. An open-ended account, is revolving credit that you can borrow, pay back, then borrow again. Credit card accounts are the most common types of open-ended debt. Below is a chart, listing the statute of limitations by state for all four categories.

Alabama Oral- 6 Written- 6 Promissory- 6 Open- 3	Indiana Oral- 6 Written- 10 Promissory- 10 Open- 6	Nebraska Oral- 4 Written- 5 Promissory- 5 Open- 4	South Carolina Oral- 3 Written- 3 Promissory- 3 Open- 3

Alaska Oral- 6 Written- 6 Promissory- Open-	Iowa Oral- 5 Written- 10 Promissory- 5 Open- 5	Nevada Oral- 4 Written- 6 Promissory- 3 Open- 4	South Dakota Oral- 3 Written- 6 Promissory- 6 Open- 6
Arizona Oral- 3 Written- 5 Promissory- 6 Open- 3	Kansas Oral- 3 Written- 5 Promissory- 5 Open- 3	New Hampshire Oral- 3 Written- 3 Promissory- 6 Open- 3	Tennessee Oral- 6 Written- 6 Promissory- 6 Open- 6
Arkansas Oral- 3 Written- 6 Promissory- 3 Open- 3	Kentucky Oral- 5 Written- 10 Promissory- 15 Open- 5	New Jersey Oral- 6 Written- 6 Promissory- 6 Open- 6	Texas Oral- 4 Written- 4 Promissory- 4 Open- 4
California Oral- 2 Written- 4 Promissory- 4 Open- 4	Louisiana Oral- 10 Written- 10 Promissory- 10 Open- 3	New Mexico Oral- 4 Written- 6 Promissory- 6 Open- 4	Utah Oral- 4 Written- 6 Promissory- 6 Open- 4
Colorado Oral- 6 Written- 6 Promissory- 6 Open- 6	Maine Oral- 6 Written- 6 Promissory- 6 Open- 6	New York Oral- 6 Written- 6 Promissory- 6 Open- 6	Vermont Oral- 6 Written- 6 Promissory- 5 Open- 3
Connecticut Oral- 3 Written- 6 Promissory- 6 Open- 3	Maryland Oral- 3 Written- 3 Promissory- 6 Open- 3	North Carolina Oral- 3 Written- 3 Promissory- 5 Open- 3	Virginia Oral- 3 Written- 5 Promissory- 6 Open- 3
Delaware Oral- 3 Written- 3 Promissory- 3 Open- 4	Massachusetts Oral- 6 Written- 6 Promissory- 6 Open- 6	North Dakota Oral- 6 Written- 6 Promissory- 6 Open- 6	Washington Oral- 3 Written- 6 Promissory- 6 Open- 3
Florida Oral- 4 Written- 5 Promissory- 5 Open- 4	Michigan Oral- 6 Written- 6 Promissory- 6 Open- 6	Ohio Oral- 15 Written- 15 Promissory- 15 Open- 6	West Virginia Oral- 5 Written- 10 Promissory- 6 Open- 5
Georgia Oral- 4 Written- 6 Promissory- 6 Open- 6	Minnesota Oral- 6 Written- 6 Promissory- 6 Open- 6	Oklahoma Oral- 3 Written- 5 Promissory- 5 Open- 3	Wisconsin Oral- 6 Written- 6 Promissory- 10 Open- 6
Hawaii Oral- 6 Written- 6 Promissory- 6 Open- 6	Mississippi Oral- 3 Written- 3 Promissory- 3 Open- 3	Oregon Oral- 6 Written- 6 Promissory- 6 Open- 6	Wyoming Oral- 8 Written- 10 Promissory- 10 Open- 8
Idaho	Missouri	Pennsylvania	

Oral- 4 Written- 5 Promissory- 5 Open- 5	Oral- 5 Written- 10 Promissory- 10 Open- 5	Oral- 4 Written- 4 Promissory- 4 Open- 4	
Illinois Oral- 5 Written- 10 Promissory- 10 Open- 5	Montana Oral- 5 Written- 8 Promissory- 8 Open- 5	Rhode Island Oral- 10 Written- 10 Promissory- 10 Open- 10	Source www.thebalance.com; 2017

Chapter 7: Knowing Your Rights

All collection agencies are covered by the Federal Debt Collection Practices Act (FCPA) (15 U.S.C. Number 1692 and following). Under this law, collection agencies cannot partake in any illegal activity. They can be sued by you if they violate any part of the act. Some states have added to these laws in order to further protect you. If you know your rights and in the likely event that a collection agency disobeys either of the federal or state laws, you will not feel intimated when the collection agency employs any illegal means. You can benefit from negotiations with the creditor depending on which law the agency disobeys. You can also press for damages by filing a complaint with the Federal Trade Commission against the collector, or sue both the creditor and the collection agency, if both of them violate the law. You may reach an agreement with the creditor not to sue if the creditor's behavior was grossly offensive, but he has agreed to remove any negative remarks from your credit report.

What to do if You are Sued

Usually, the first indication that you are being sued is when you receive a complaint and/or a summons. The complaint describes the nature and dollar amount of the claims against you for your unpaid debt. The summons is a written letter notifying you that you are required to appear in court on a specific date if you want to defend yourself against the claim. If you simply ignore the complaint by not replying with a formal answer, your inaction may result in a default judgment against you. If you decide to go without an attorney, which is understandable depending on the specifics of your case or personal financial means, you should read up on court procedures in your state and gather the forms you will need.

A creditor suing you for an unpaid debt also must be able to document ownership of the debt. Creditors usually sell debts to debt collectors for legal purposes. They must be able to produce documented proof of the debt in order to sue you, a requirement that does not apply to the original creditor. You should request verification of the debt in writing once you are contacted by a debt collector. If they cannot provide written verification, they cannot legally collect from you. Like I've stated in a previous chapter, if you feel like something isn't right, don't be afraid to fight it. The biggest danger when it comes to being sued is doing nothing. 80% of those sued by original creditors do nothing. If you do nothing, you will lose, and the creditor/plaintiff will get a default judgment against you.

Tips for Representing Yourself in Court

1. Dress appropriately. Never wear denim, or loud colors. Always make sure your shirts and blouses are tucked in. Men be sure to wear a professional looking tie and court appropriate shoes. Ladies make sure your skirts are no shorter than knee length. Try to keep your hair as neat as possible.

2. Keep a trial notebook. During your trial, you'll probably give your own testimony, question witnesses and present arguments about why you should win the case. Writing down what you want to ask, say and how you want to approach these questions can be very beneficial to winning your case. You can use a simple three-ring binder with tabs for each section.

3. Watch some trials on television or YouTube. Before your case comes up for trial, go down to the courthouse and sit in on a couple of trials involving similar issues. You'll see that it won't be that difficult to present your story and your

proven fact that when you send a copy of the credit report which contains the disputed items, it gives better results.

Templates

When it comes to writing a letter of reinvestigation, like any letter involving credit repair, you must customize it to fit your situation, while still maintaining professionalism. *Pro tip: Use these as a guideline template below and customize them to fit your current situation.** The first, is a letter to request an investigation. The second, is a letter to file a complaint. **Please remember to attach copies of your social security card, and driver's license/ID cards.**

Jessica Baxter

123 Main Street apt# 222

Dallas, TX 75204

555-78-9876

Oct. 6, 1987

10/30/2017

Dear Equifax

I have reviewed my report recently. There are addresses, names that are incorrect - spelling errors or just plain wrong. PLEASE fix EVERYTHING in my personal information that is NOT the following:

1.Name: This is my legal name: JESSICA BAXTER. Please delete any other references to names as they are not mine and I have never used any of them.
Jessie M. Baxter
Jessica L. Braxton

2. Address: Also, please be sure that my address is listed correctly. My address should read 123 MAIN ST APT 222, DALLAS TX 75204. Please remove all other addresses on my report, as they are NOT deliverable to me by US Post Office, and they are reportable as per the FCRA since they are inaccurate.
2411 N PRAIRIE AVE
3535 201 MUNGER AVE
2630 HOUSE GHENT ST
1722 ATLAS DR

Please delete all accounts that are associated with this inaccurate information immediately. Send me a new report which includes my personal profile when you are completed so that I may verify its' accuracy.

Thank you

Your Full Name (Make sure it matches the name on your credit report)
Address
City, State Zip
SSN: 000-00-0000 | DOB: 7/1/1960

June 1, 2013

Equifax
P.O. Box 740256
Atlanta, GA 30374

This letter is to inform you that I recently received a copy of my credit report that your company publishes and after reviewing it I found a number of items on the report that are inaccurate. The accounts in question are listed below.

Please send me copies of the documents that you have in your files as of this date that you used to verify the accuracy of the accounts listed below.

Under the Fair Credit Reporting Act, **15 U.S.C. § 1681g** I have the right to demand that you disclose to me all of the documents that you have recorded and retained in your file at the time of this request concerning the accounts that you are reporting in my credit report. Please don't respond to my request by saying that these accounts have been verified. Send me copies of the documents that you have in your files that were used to verify them.

If you do not have any documentation in your files to verify the accuracy of these disputed accounts then please delete them immediately as required under **Section 611(a)(5)(A)(i).** By publishing these inaccurate and unverified items on my credit report and distributing them to 3rd parties you are damaging my reputation and credit worthiness.

Under the **FCRA 15 U.S.C. § 1681i**, all **unverified accounts must be promptly deleted**. Therefore, if you are unable to provide me with a copy of the verifiable proof that you have on file for each of the accounts listed below within 30 days of receipt of this letter then you must remove these accounts from my credit report.

Please provide me with a copy of an updated and corrected credit report showing these items removed.

I demand the following accounts be properly verified or removed immediately.

Name of Account:	Account Number:	Provide Physical Proof of Verification
1. Chase Bank	#533376304023 ...	Unverified Account

(Hand Write this information with blue ink pen)
Make sure that you don't have more than 22 accounts listed

* **NOTE: Please also remove all non-account holding inquiries over 30 days old.**

Thank You,

Sign your name here

(Your Name Here)

August 1, 2013

'our Name
ıddress
:ity, State Zip
;SN: 000-00-0000 | DOB: 1/1/1960

:quifax
'.O. Box 740256
ıtlanta, GA 30374

Please be advised that this is my <u>SECOND WRITTEN REQUEST</u> asking you to remove the nverified accounts listed below that remain on my credit report in violation of 15 U.S.C. § 1681. 'ou are required under the FCRA to have properly verified the accuracy of an account listed on ny credit report. In the results of your first re-investigation, you stated in writing that you **verified"** that these items are being **"reported correctly".**

Where **are the documents that you used to verify these accounts? Vhat is the name of the person <u>in your company</u> who verified these accounts? Vhat documents did they use to verify them? Please provide me with the name f that individual, their business address, and telephone number.**

Black's Law Dictionary, 9th Edition, 2009, defines "**Verify**" as, 1) "To prove to be true; o confirm or establish the truth or truthfulness of; to authenticate." 2) "to confirm or substantiate by ath or affidavit; to swear to the truth of." and **"Verification" as, "Confirmation of correctness, ruth or authenticity, by affidavit, oath, or deposition. Affidavit of truth of a matter stated nd object of verification is to assure good faith in averments or statements of a party."** Vhat this means is that your company must be willing and able to produce a document in our files that proves the account(s) in dispute belong to me and the information being reported s accurate and you must be able to do this in a court of law if I file a lawsuit against you. ;omeone in your company must authenticate the documents in your files that were used to erify the disputed accounts and to do this they must have 1st hand knowledge of the alleged ccount(s) and all that has ever transpired for the alleged account(s), under oath and under the enalty of perjury. As I am sure that you are well aware, current Federal case law states that, ***:onsumer Reporting Agencies bear grave responsibilities to ensure the accuracy of the ccounts they report on and their responsibility must consist of something more than nerely parroting information received from other sources.*** The Courts have also ordered hat **a "Reinvestigation" that merely shifts the burden back to the consumer and the redit grantor cannot fulfill the obligations imposed by § 1681(a)(4).**

You have ignored my request to provided me with the documents that you have in your les that you used to verify the disputed accounts which means that you have NOT verified or ou cannot verify any of these accounts and under **Section 611 (5)(A**) of the FCRA – ou are required to ***"...promptly DELETE all information which cannot be verified."*** 'he law is very clear as to the Civil liability and the remedy available to me for negligent noncompliance" **Section 617**) if you fail to comply with this Federal Law. **I am a litigious consumer nd fully intend on pursuing litigation in this matter to enforce my rights under the FCRA. demand the following accounts be verified or deleted immediately.**

<u>Name of Account</u>:	<u>Account Number</u>:	<u>Provide Physical Proof of Verification</u>
1. Chase Bank	#533376304023 ...	Unverified Account

(Hand Write this information with blue ink pen)

Note: If they have already removed some of the items that you listed on your first letter than remove them from your list on this letter.

On removal of the above noted accounts please provide me with a copy of an updated and corrected copy of my credit report showing that these accounts have been removed.

Thanking you in advance for your anticipated quick co-operation on this matter.

Thank you,

Your Signature Here

Your Name Here

August 1, 2013

'our Name
\ddress
;ity, State Zip
;SN: 000-00-0000 | DOB: 1/1/1970

Equifax
P.O. Box 740256
Atlanta, GA 30374

Please be advised that this is my THIRD WRITTEN REQUEST and 'INAL WARNING that I fully intend to pursue litigation in accordance with the 'CRA to enforce my rights and seek relief and recover all monetary damages hat I may be entitled to under Section 616 and Section 617 regarding your :ontinued willful and negligent noncompliance.

Despite my previous 2 written requests, the unverified items listed below still emain on my credit report in violation of Federal Law. You stated in your responses ɔ my 2 dispute letters that you have verified that the items listed below are accurate ›ut you failed to send me copies of the documents that you used to verify these ıccounts as per my request. The fact that you have ignored my request to send me :opies of the documents that you used to verify the disputed accounts is evidence ıat you cannot and did not verify any of the disputed accounts like you said you did. 'our failure to delete the disputed accounts that you can not verify after two written 'equests is also evidence of your willful disregard of Federal Law. When we go to itigation and through the discovery process you will be required to produce these locuments along with an affidavit swearing under oath that these are the true and :orrect documents that you used to verify the disputed accounts. The fact that you lon't have any of the said documents in your files is proof that you did not properly erify the accounts within 30 days as required by law and the Court will order you to lelete them.

You say that you have reinvestigated these accounts but you've admitted that ıll you have done is parroted information given to you by other sources and shifted ıe burden back to me to contact the original creditor to verify these accounts which is :learly in violation of § 1681(a)(4). I also asked you to give me the name of the person in our company who verified the accuracy of these accounts but you ignored this request ıs well which is another violation of Federal Law and evidence of your willful disregard of the law.

Please be advised that under **Section 611 (5)(A)** of the FCRA – you are required to *'...promptly DELETE all information which cannot be verified."* I request that you do this nmediately. The law is very clear as to the Civil liability and the remedy available to me **Section 616 & 617**) if you fail to comply with Federal Law. I am a litigious consumer ınd fully intend on pursuing litigation in this matter to enforce my rights under the FCRA.

demand that you delete all of the accounts listed below immediately. 'lease provide me with a copy of an updated and corrected credit eport showing that these items have been deleted.

Name of Account:	Account Number:	Provide Physical Proof of Verification
1. Chase Bank	#533376304023 ...	Unverified Account

(Hand Write this information with blue ink pen)

Note: If they have already removed some of the items that you listed on your first & second letter than remove them from your list on this letter.

Thanking you in advance for your anticipated quick co-operation on this matter.
Thank you,
Your Signature Here

Your Name Here
Attached: Copy of my Social Security Card & Drivers License is attached
Sent: USPS Certified Mail

Chapter 9: Building and Budgeting

So far, I have given you detailed insight on how credit works, steps toward rebuilding, and the ins and outs of dealing with creditors. But your spending and saving habits are what will truly keep you on the right path to improving your financial future. In this part, I will be giving you some helpful tips on how to budget and save.

Budgeting Your Money

If you use cash, the envelope method is where you put a specific amount of money in an envelope for spending. It can be your bills, your groceries or even spending money (if you can properly fit it into your budget.) After the money in the envelope is gone, that's it! Taking a few hours every weekend to grocery shop and meal plan for the week will definitely help you budget your money, as dining out is the No. 1 expense for most people. By eating at home, you save money that would otherwise be spent on tax and tip. Buying your household necessities at the nearby dollar stores can cut down on your monthly spending, as well as couponing to cut down on these items and your groceries. Making a schedule and sticking to it, can also improve your monthly expenses. Set up auto drafts out of your checking account to pay bills and buy your groceries on a set day every week or twice a month. When you know what to expect and when to expect it, you take a lot of stress and potential pitfalls out of the picture. Writing things down has become quite an old-fashioned way of helping you stay on track with your goals and keeping you organized. Keeping a journal or writing things down on a calendar can help you plan when you're going to pay bills, and what expenses should remain a priority. During this time, update your budget, review your accounts and track your progress against your financial goals. Like any relationship, if you want your financial life to improve, you must spend time with your money. It usually takes three to four months to get accustomed to a habit, so don't give up. Things may feel tight, but you'll get used to it in no time.

Whenever you're attempting to make a significant change in your life, things can become frustrating, and take a toll on you emotionally. Look to your spouse, your parents, or your closest friends for help or support. Surrounding yourself with people who have positive spending habits and a healthy financial life will encourage you to want better for yourself. When you surround yourself with people who have negative spending habits, they just encourage you to spend frivolously. I know it stings to sacrifice those Friday night outings, but you won't regret it in the long run.

Saving your Money

Still paying for cable? Why? With online streaming services, you have endless entertainment for less than twenty dollars a month. While streaming requires internet service, the average American most likely pays for internet service anyway. With cutting the cable cord, you're paying for one less financial burden while still getting to watch most of your favorite shows. Make a weekly "money date." Depending on where you live, letting your car sit home and catching the public bus a few days out of the week can help you save at least half of your transportation budget, by not needing to purchase gas. If you're paying a monthly fee for your checking or savings account, you would benefit from researching different types of banking offers from other banks. Not only do some of the banks offer sign-up bonuses simply for opening an account and setting up direct deposit, but some offer attractive interest rates to new customers as well.

Have you ever heard of the 30-day rule? Have you ever seen an item on Amazon that you just had to have, but instead of buying it right away, you put it on your wish list? I'm sure you have, we all have. But how many times have you scrolled past that item on your wish list, only to realize you no longer wanted it? Well that's how the 30-day rule works. The idea is that you wait at least 30 days to purchase an item. This way, the urge to buy it will most likely pass by then. This is a helpful way to avoid impulse purchases.

I get it, you want to enjoy life, but still get your finances and credit right. No one likes the idea of sitting home every weekend while their friends and family enjoy nights out and fun trips. But the struggle will be worth it when you're able to afford that nice new car without the high interest rate. Or when you can finally buy that house for your children to grow up in. This is why I previously stressed how important it is to have a positive and healthy support system while going through the process of credit repair. Sometimes you will be tempted, and sometimes you may cave in. Nobody is perfect, not even me. Just remember that saving money is never a waste of time and will always be a necessity no matter how good or bad your credit is.

Conclusion

I hope that by reading this book, you were able to take in vital information to prepare yourself for a future with better credit. My goal is for you to take this information and to flourish, having the things in life that you deserve, without a negative credit score or report holding you back. Never think that it is too late for you to fix your credit. I've seen the worst, and I've been the worst in terms of an atrocious score. The path to better credit does not happen overnight. It can be a long, daunting and tedious process, but those of us at Wealthy Rise Credit Solutions are here as a support system for getting you back on track! Visit my website **www.wealthyrise.com** today or visit Facebook.com today and join my group, *Building Credit & Wealth*. We are a supportive group that uplifts and encourages our members. Learn how to fix bad credit, rebuild credit, use credit to build wealth, change your life. How to get approved for you dream house or car, FREE tips and financial information! All directly from me, Latrice Douglas, the CEO of Wealthy Rise Credit Solutions LLC. "Keep your credit on the RISE!"

Glossary

APR
The annual percentage rate (APR) is the simplified counterpart to the effective interest rate that the borrower will pay on a loan.

Annual Fee
Any fee that is charged on an annual (yearly) basis.

Balance
In a margin account, is the amount of funds deposited in the customer's account following the successful execution of a short sale order.

Bankruptcy
A legal status of a person or other entity that cannot repay debts to creditors.

Charge Off
The declaration by a creditor (usually a credit card account) that an amount of debt is unlikely to be collected.

Civil Action
Any court action against a consumer to regain money for someone else. Usually, it will be a wage assignment, child support judgment, small claims judgment or a civil judgment.

Claims
An application for compensation under the terms of an insurance policy.

Commission
An amount of money, typically a set percentage of the value involved, paid to an agent in a commercial transaction.

Consumer Report
Any written, oral, or other communication of any information by a consumer reporting agency bearing on a consumer's credit worthiness, credit standing, credit capacity, character, general reputation, personal characteristics, or mode of living which is used or expected to be used or collected in whole or in part for the purpose of serving as a factor in establishing the consumer's eligibility.

Cosigner
Person who pledges in writing as part of a credit contract to repay the debt if the borrower fails to do so. The account displays on both the borrower's and the cosigner's credit reports.

Creditor
A person or company to whom money is owed.

Credit Monitoring
A credit monitoring service allows you to keep the closest eye possible on your credit. You can

check your credit score as often as you like and track changes in your credit report from each of the three credit bureaus.

Credit Risk
The chance of loss due to a borrower's defaulting on a loan or not meeting contractual obligations.

Credit Worthiness
An assessment of a prospective borrower to determine the likelihood that the borrower will default on debts.

Debt
Something owed by one party, the borrower or debtor, to a second party, the lender or creditor.

Debt Consolidation
A form of debt refinancing that entails taking out one loan to pay off many others.

Default
Failure to meet the legal obligations (or conditions) of a loan.

Delinquency
Refers to accounts that are not paid on time.

Dispute
A written document sent from a borrower to their lender or to a credit bureau/agency.

DOLA
Date of last Activity; The date when one of three things happens on any active account: the consumer makes a payment, misses a payment, or the balance of the account increases.

FACTA
Fair and Accurate Credit Transactions Act; The law provided, among other things, additional protections for consumers in connection with the prevention and remediation of identity theft and the accuracy of credit reports.

FCBA
Fair Credit Billing Act; This act requires prompt written acknowledgment of consumer billing complaints and investigation of billing errors by creditors.

FCRA
Fair Credit Reporting Act (effective April 25, 1971); is part of a group of acts in the Federal Consumer Credit Protection Act. The Act protects information collected by consumer reporting agencies such as credit bureaus, medical information companies and tenant screening services.

FDCPA
Fair Debt Collection Practices Act; Under this Act (Title VIII of the Consumer Credit Protection Act), third-party debt collectors are prohibited from employing deceptive or abusive conduct in

the collection of consumer debts incurred for personal, family, or household purposes.

FICO®

A FICO® score is a credit score produced from models developed by Fair Isaac Corporation. The score is used to measure a consumer's creditworthiness and risk and is in use worldwide.

Finance Charges

The amount you are charged to use credit.

Fluctuations

An irregular rising and falling in number or amount; a variation.

Judgements

a court order that gives a creditor the legal right to collect from a debtor.

HIPPA

Health Insurance Portability and Accountability Act; passed by Congress in 1996. HIPAA Mandates industry-wide standards for health care information on electronic billing and other processes; and requires the protection and confidential handling of protected health information.

Inquiry

An examination of a consumer's credit history. When your credit report is made available to another party, such as a lender, landlord or insurer.

Installment Loan
A credit account in which the amount of the payment and the number of payments are predetermined or fixed.

Interest
The cost of borrowing or lending money, usually a percentage of the amount borrowed or loaned.
Interest Rate
A percentage of money charged by a lender, for borrowing money.

Line of Credit
Credit limit established by a creditor.

Principal Balance
Account principal and other legally collectible costs, expenses, and interest accrued prior to the Charge off Date, less payments or settlements since charge off, if any.

Repossession
Repossession is a term used to denote a financial institution taking back an object that was either used as collateral or rented or leased.

Revolving Credit

An account that requires at least a specified minimum payment each month plus a service charge on the balance, which can fluctuate up to the credit limit. As the balance declines, the amount of the service charge, or interest, also declines.

Secured credit card
A credit that requires a cash deposit. Generally, the amount of the deposit is equal to the credit line.

Settlement
Payment of the adjustment amount of an account, including principal, interest and fees.

Tax Lien
A charge upon real or personal property for the satisfaction of debts related to taxes.

Term
The amount of time in which a loan must be repaid in full.

VantageScores
This is a score created by the three major credit reporting bureaus in 2006, aimed at competing with the FICO® Score. You can purchase your VantageScores through Experian, TransUnion, and Equifax.

Variable Rate
A variable rate is an interest rate that may fluctuate over the life of a loan, typically in response to changes in the interest rate marketplace.

This book was published by Wealthy Rise Credit Solutions, LLC

Don't forget to visit wealthyrise.com and follow *Building Credit & Wealth on* Facebook! Thanks for reading!

Made in the USA
Monee, IL
04 November 2026

67378313R00056